james blunt
back to bedlam

© 2006 by International Music Publications Ltd
First published in 2006 by International Music Publications Ltd
International Music Publications Ltd is a Faber Music company
3 Queen Square, London WC1N 3AU

Cover by Salvador Design
Artwork & Design by Bose Collins Ltd & James Blunt
Illustration by Matt Durston
Photography by Steve Double, Lynn Campbell & Cyndi Sayre

Arranged by Chris Hussey
Engraved by Camden Music
Edited by Lucy Holliday
Printed in England by Caligraving Ltd
All rights reserved

ISBN 0-571-52541-5

To buy Faber Music publications or to find out about the full range of
titles available, please contact your local music retailer or Faber Music sales enquiries:
Faber Music Ltd, Burnt Mill, Elizabeth Way, Harlow, CM20 2HX England
Tel: +44 (0) 1279 82 89 82   Fax: +44 (0) 1279 82 89 83
sales@fabermusic.com   fabermusic.com

back to bedlam

www.jamesblunt.com

High

Words and Music by James Blunt and Ricky Ross

You're Beautiful

Words and Music by James Blunt, Sacha Skarbek and Amanda Ghost

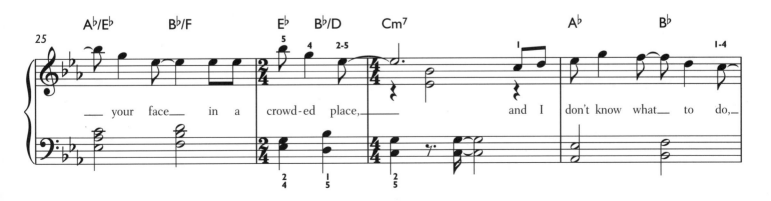

Wisemen

Words and Music by James Blunt, Jimmy Hogarth and Sacha Skarbek

Goodbye My Lover

Words and Music by James Blunt and Sacha Skarbek

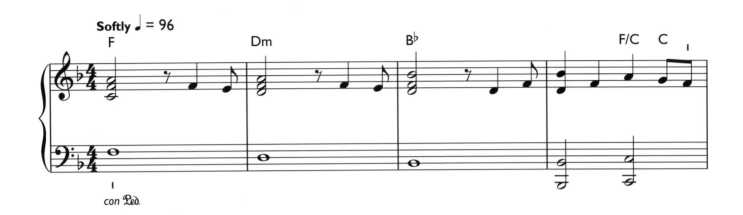

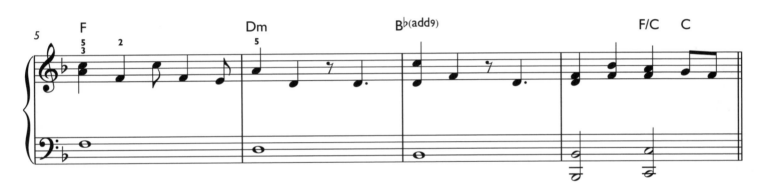

Did I dis-ap-point you,   or let you down?____   Should I be feel-ing guil-ty,

or let the jud-ges frown?   'Cause I saw the end be-fore we'd be-gun,____ yes I

Tears And Rain

Words and Music by Guy Chambers and James Blunt

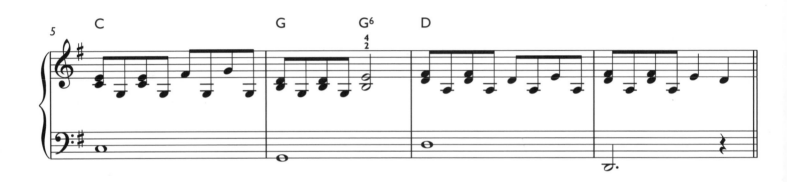

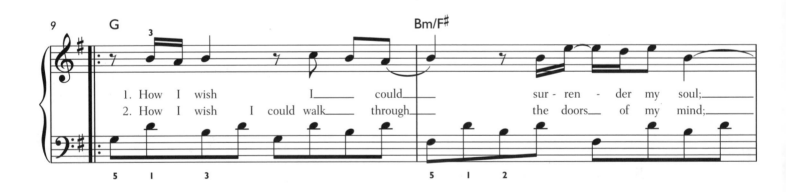

Out Of My Mind

Words and Music by James Blunt

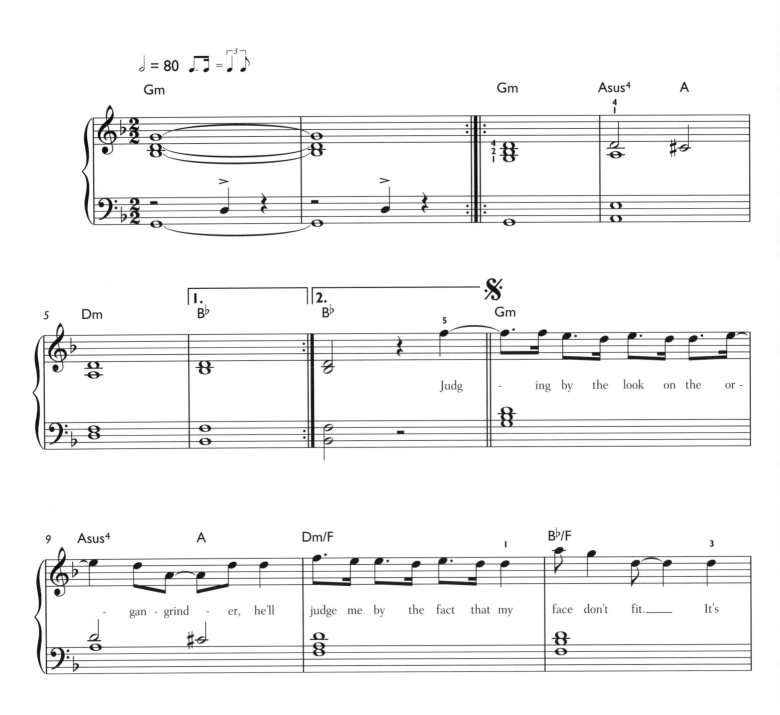

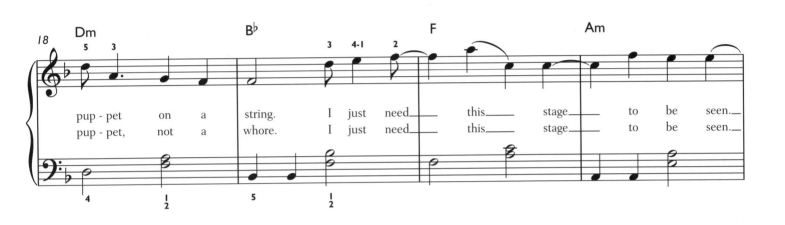

30

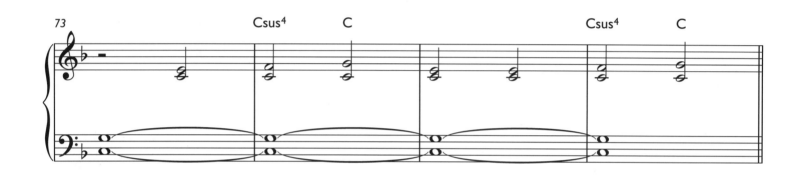

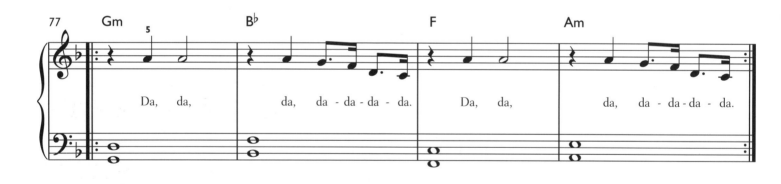

So Long, Jimmy

Words and Music by James Blunt and Jimmy Hogarth

1. I just can't be - lieve___ that it's o - ver.___
2. I'm just so re - lieved___ that it's o - ver.___

Billy

Words and Music by James Blunt, Sacha Skarbek and Amanda Ghost

1. Bil - ly's leav - ing to - day,
2. Bil - ly's leav - ing to - day,

(don't know where he's go - ing).
(don't know where he's go - ing).

Holds his head in dis - grace,
He's got lines on his face,

(he can't es - cape the truth).
(they tell the sto - ry of his pain).

He knows the price that he's paid.
He ac - cepts it's his fate.

He ad - mits that it's too
He ad - mits it took too

late to ad - mit that he's a -
long to ad - mit that he was

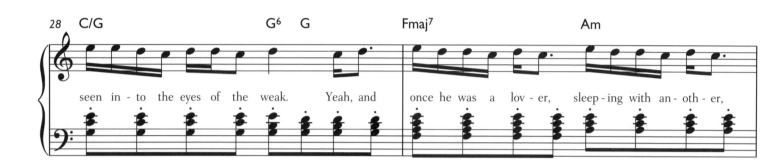

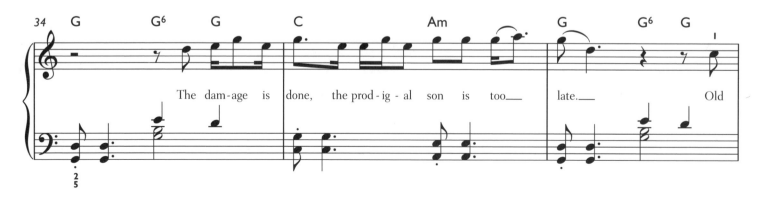

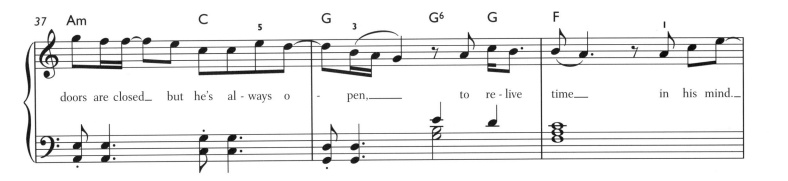

doors are closed__ but he's al - ways o - pen,____ to re - live time__ in his mind.__

__ Oh Bil - ly. Oh Bil - ly.__

__ Ooh,_____

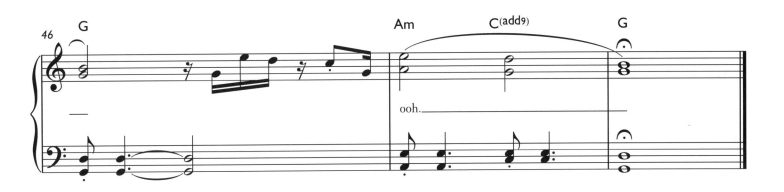

__ ooh._____

Cry

Words and Music by James Blunt and Sacha Skarbek

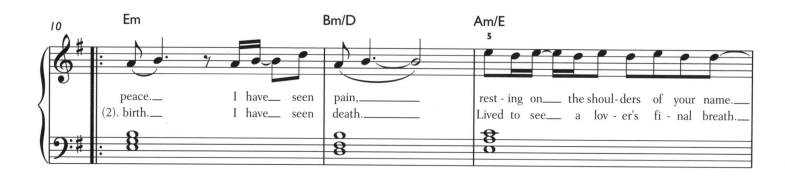

No Bravery

Words and Music by James Blunt and Sacha Skarbek

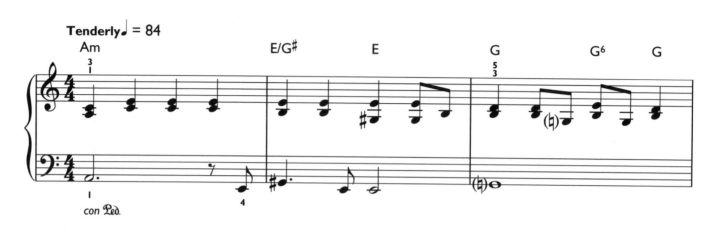

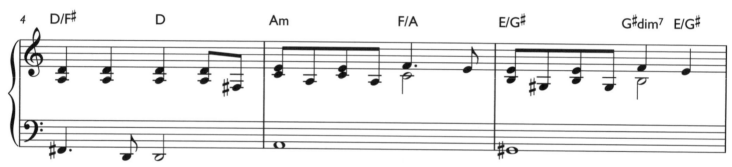

1. There are child - ren stand - ing here,
3. There are child - ren stand - ing here,

arms out - stretched in - to the sky,___ tears___ dry - ing on___ their face,___
arms out - stretched in - to the sky,___ but no - one asks___ the ques - tion why,___

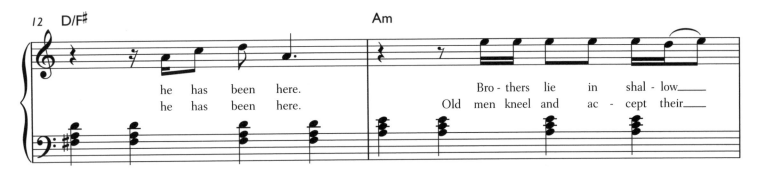

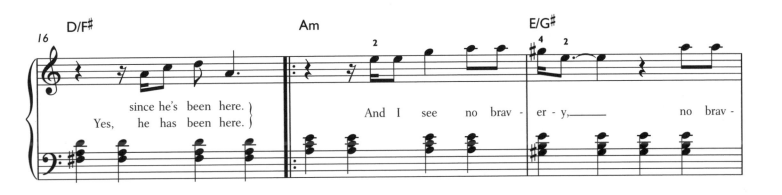

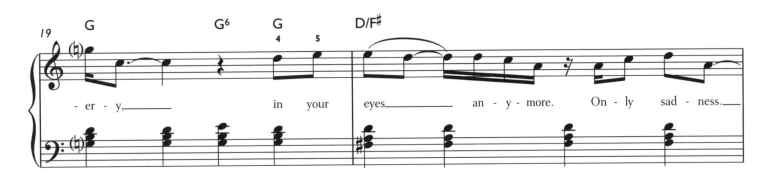

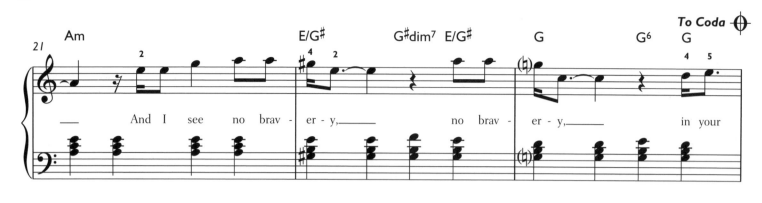

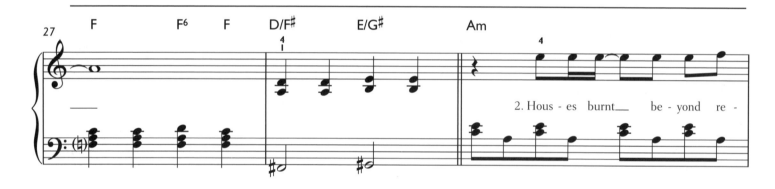

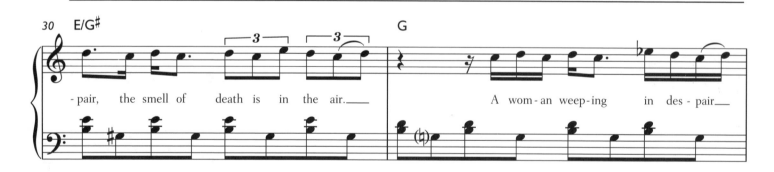

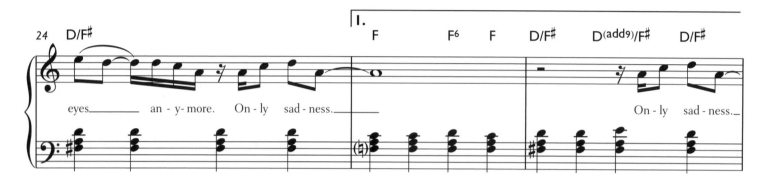

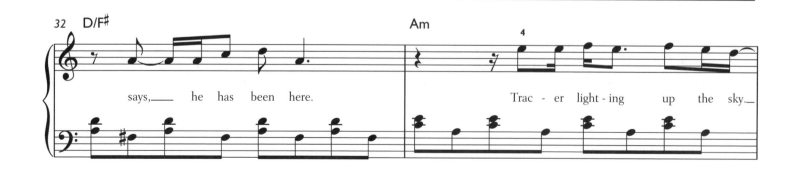

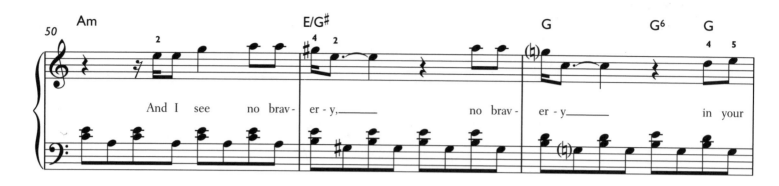

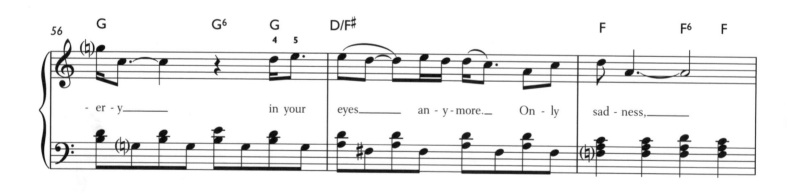